I0476476

The "Outside the Box" Entrepreneur

The Mindset, Marketing and Making of YOUR Lifestyle Business

Alicia Cramer

For general inquiries contact Alicia Cramer at (888) 608-1778 or email support@aliciacramer.com

ISBN-13: 978-1511965606

ISBN-10: 1511965606

Contents

Preface

Who this book is for:

This book is for the professional service provider who has built a successful brick and mortar business, but is not satisfied with the long hours, huge overhead and demands of running a professional practice. They are tired and unfulfilled and have committed to enjoy life more.

This book is for the business owner who is an entrepreneur at heart, but has become enslaved by their business and is falling out of love with it. They are fed up, and seek to create a business that supports them emotionally and financially.

This book is for the entrepreneur who is almost there... they have the passion, vision and discipline, but something is holding them back from the real wealth and fulfillment they desire. They know something must change, and they are determined to succeed.

This book is for you if you want more out of life. If you have the DNA of an entrepreneur, yet find yourself bumping up against an invisible wall. Perhaps you have successfully grown your business (or even many businesses), but you are unfulfilled. *You have called this book into your life because you are ready to make a change.* The time is now; and if you just said yes to yourself, then you are ready... let's get started.

What this book is about:

This book addresses the mindset that goes along with creating a business and life you love. It is based on principles you may have studied in classic books, like Think and Grow Rich. And it is touches on the science of the mind; how we can recondition our beliefs and behaviors to achieve greater success and fulfillment. It also intertwines strategies and concepts for creating real – tangible business results based on your lifestyle goals. .. But in a slightly out of the box way.

With complete transparency I can say that I've fallen into each category described in the *Who this book is for section*. In fact, I have found that you never "arrive" at success. You will continue to stretch… to achieve what's desired, then reach for more, better, and different. It is a part of life and a part of business. While I do not profess to be a guru, the principles I share in this book have continued to serve me over the years. They are a foundation that I frequently revisit as I grow, evolve and change. And have shared them with my clients for years. Now it is my intention to share them with you, so you can benefit from them as well.

There is no doubt that this book can be transformational for some readers. For most, it will be about refinement. Subtle shifts that you can create in your mind, and in your business, to be and do and have a life and business that is more empowering and fulfilling.

For best results, use this book like you would a workbook. Complete the recommended activities. Answer the questions as honestly as you can. Be proactive (not passive). And revisit the book at various points in the future when you are up leveling your life and/or business again.

If you feel inspired to work with me one-on-one, schedule a complimentary phone consultation at:

www.aliciacramer.com

> *Thinking outside the box (also thinking out of the box or thinking beyond the box) is a metaphor that means to think differently, unconventionally, or from a new perspective. This phrase often refers to novel or creative thinking.*

Chapter 1

What do you really want?

Several years ago I developed a group coaching program called Business Mindset Mastery. It was designed for new to intermediate business owners who hadn't fully embodied the core traits of successful entrepreneurs. You are already well aware that there is a significant difference between an entrepreneurial mindset and an employee mentality. And for most business owners, there is a process that must be gone through to develop those mindset traits.

The very first concept I addressed with my students in that program begins with this question: **What do you really want?** Followed by an honest assessment of why?

Most of us think we know what we want and why. But I challenge you, be very honest with yourself. Do you *really* know what you want in your life and business? Why do you believe you want *it*?

From the time we are born (some say even while in utero) we are absorbing, learning and forming conclusions about life from people around us. We begin to take on certain points of view about what success is. And most people are creating their lives based on other people's beliefs about what you should or should not do – on what other people believe success is.

Pause to answer the following questions:

- What do you believe success is?

- Where did those beliefs come from?

- Does your version of what success is align with what you really, truly, want for your life?

Chances are, if you have any degree of un-fulfillment in your life and/or business, your current beliefs are not completely aligned with what you truly want to experience in your life.

The *first step* is to be honest about what you want and make a decision to have it. The *second step* is to get aligned and take action to create it.

Having a lifestyle business does not mean you rarely work (unless of course that is your goal). The online marketing boom exploited the idea of sitting on the beach with your laptop working a few hours a week while millions of dollars roll in.

Let's cut the BS, real entrepreneurs work... But, they love what they do. In many cases, they work long and hard because they love it. Being a lifestyle entrepreneur is about aligning your day-to-day week-to-week and month-to-month activities with the lifestyle you prefer. And do it in a strategic way that that allows you to achieve your financial goals.

Chapter 2

Getting Aligned

As a Business Coach and Mindset Strategist (a word I coined to describe the unique way I work with clients to shift subconscious patterns), I help my clients identify and resolve the old beliefs/patterns that create problems in their life. We all have beliefs, behavior patterns, unresolved emotional wounds and fears that hold us back from the happiness, fulfillment and success we aspire for. This is where the misalignment originates.

In order to create what we want in life or business, we must be in alignment with it. When our old conditioning opposes our desire, the achievement of our desire can feel impossible.

Virtually every one of us can relate to setting a goal that was easy for us to achieve. Likewise, we can all relate to setting a goal that not only seemed to elude us, but was extremely emotionally painful in the striving (and potentially failing) to achieve it.

It always has to do with our beliefs, or what I refer to as our conditioning.

This understanding of belief systems has become common knowledge to many. You don't have to attend college for psychology or receive advanced training in hypnotherapy from an accredited collage like I did to understand that our beliefs affect our lives. That being said, understanding how to change your belief systems is much more complex. Furthermore, the answer to our greatest challenge is typically in our blind spot. Sometimes we need help to clearly see what is holding us back.

What is alignment?

I frequently use the word alignment. It has a metaphysical origin, as well as a practical one. I believe both are relevant. We live in a fascinating universe; complex beyond comprehension. It is perfect – infallible – strategic – mathematical and adhering to strict universal laws that govern our existence. If that seemed deep, that was my intention. To understand alignment, we must understand the law of attraction. A senior law, which encompasses several other universal principles, and can be simply defined as: **Like Attracts Like.**

Metaphysicians long before our time knew that everything in our universe is energy. Everything seen and unseen vibrates at different frequencies. Whether it is the chair you are sitting on, the electromagnetic frequency emitted by your cellphone, or the thoughts you are thinking, they are all energy; each vibrating at a unique frequency. Taking this concept a step further, each thought you think has its own unique frequency. And their corresponding emotions are also vibrational in nature.

The law of attraction could be explained metaphorically as the law of magnetism. The magnet is always either attracting or repelling based on its polarity. It doesn't stop. Again, it is always working – either attracting or repelling. Forgive my seeming insensitivity towards ignorance, but anyone who says the law of attraction doesn't work for them is wrong. It is a law, it is always working. You are always attracting to you a vibrational match to your dominant thought/emotion vibrations.

So when I refer to alignment, I am referring to a state of being. Specifically, when your dominate thought-emotion vibration is aligned with the vibration of what you want.

When you have old beliefs, patterns, and conditioning that contradict what you desire, you are emitting a vibrational frequency that is out of alignment. Like the magnet in our metaphor, it is repelling what you want.

An important caveat: It is not always necessary, and certainly not beneficial to try to identify and change every "negative" belief or pattern. It is, however, necessary and beneficial when you know you are out of alignment with what you desire. Especially when the thing you wish to change is creating distress.

When you have old beliefs, patterns, and conditioning that contradict what you desire, you are emitting a vibrational frequency that is out of alignment.

How to release the beliefs, patterns and conditioning that are creating misalignment?

This is a big topic. One so big, there are literally millions of books, audios, therapists, coaches, experts, programs, and techniques to address it. *Is there one that is more effective than another?* Sure. *Is there one that is guaranteed to work for everyone?* Unlikely. Why it is that way is another big topic, and one that I will not address here. However, I will say, in order for any technique, expert or solution to work for you, you must have made the decision to change.

I like to use an example to demonstrate this important concept. When I owned and operated my hypnotherapy practice, I attracted a lot of clients who wanted to quit smoking. Before I would agree to take on the client, I assessed their readiness to quit. Smoking is an interesting thing, because there are a lot of emotional reasons someone smokes. There are also a lot of emotional reasons that same individual wants to quit.

The subconscious mind stores all of the memories, good and bad associations, habitually practiced and reconditioned responses the smoker has had. And even when someone knows all the logical rational reasons to quit, from the health implications to the expense and social dogmas, their subconscious is holding a stronger more powerful positive association with the behavior.

The good news is that the old positive associations can be overridden. And smoking can easily become a thing of the past. But, if the individual has not make the decision to quit, if they waiver, or if they are doing it because someone else wants them to – not of their own choosing, then nothing or no one has the power to facilitate the change.

This is important to understand. You can change almost any belief, pattern or conditioning with the right tools and intention. But, if you have not decided -- if you have not committed, then you will not change. If you waiver, then you are holding onto a belief that there is more benefit to stay the same than to change.

Stop for a moment and reflect on this...

Honestly reflect on what <u>benefit</u> you get from staying the same (your current circumstances). Is it the comfort of what is known? Is there a secret benefit, like sympathy? Be brutally honest with yourself, because if you truly want to create the lifestyle you desire, and something is in the way, then you must identify what you are holding onto and be willing to release it. You must make a committed decision to change.

This is important to understand. You can change almost any belief, pattern or conditioning with the right tools and intention. But, if you have not decided – if you have not committed, then you will not change. If you waiver, then you are holding onto a belief that there is more benefit to stay the same than to change.

Review and Implementation

You already know the importance of taking action. In fact, often what separates successful individuals from those who live a life of mediocrity is the willingness to take persistent action in spite of obstacles, setbacks and delayed gratification. If you have not already taken time for introspection based on the previous chapters, I encourage you to do so now.

❖ What do you really want?

Not what you think you should want or think you should have, but what you desire with your whole heart and soul. What does that look like? What does that feel like?

❖ What benefits are you getting out of your current circumstances?

Be brutally honest with yourself. If there is something you have been struggling to change, then you are holding onto something. Why might you not want to change? What are you afraid you will lose?

❖ Make a committed decision.

If you are clear about what you really want, and you are willing to let go of what was in the way, change can happen with ease.

*The ability to change starts with a committed **decision**.*

Visualization:

A Tool for Shaping Your Life

When I was a teenager I bought a book about manifesting. The author laid out a process for training your mind to create on the energetic plane (aka mental plane), so it could then manifest on the material plane. At this point, you may be thinking I have gone too woo-woo on you. But let me assure you, there is an abundance of scientific data to back up this theory. I will remind you of our discussion about vibration; everything is energy, including what cannot be perceived with our five senses. Modern science agrees, thoughts are things, and we know that everything we create -- from art to technology -- first begins as a thought.

So, back to my book about manifestation; to create what we want in life we first create it in our minds (and with our emotions). This is often referred to as visualization. Visualization is something we can train ourselves to become proficient at.

In order to train our mind, we must enter a light meditative state. This can be induced very quickly by sitting comfortably in an upright position. Close your eyes; and with your eyes closed, roll your eyes up and towards the center of your forehead. Focus on your breathing. Be aware of the rise and fall of your chest as you breathe. Let any thoughts that enter your mind flow through quickly and easily. Do this practice for about two minutes and you will naturally enter an alpha brainwave state* which is ideal for this exercise.

Next, intentionally clear your mind. It can help to imagine a large empty white room. Here you begin practicing your visualization and creation skills.

Picture in your mind – visualize or imagine – a circle. Something very simple. Then change it to 3D. See it in your mind and examine it a little. Now, add some color. Play with the size, make it larger or smaller.

Try a couple of different shapes. Square. Pyramid.

As this becomes easier, imagine something a little more complex. Perhaps a flower, like a rose or a lily.

When you feel ready, create something even more detailed. It is easiest to transition into this by visualizing or imagining your living room, or another place you spend a lot of time and know well.

And finally, shift into creating new imagery. If you feel comfortable with your ability to visualize, you can begin to see yourself having achieved what you desire. See it, sense it, feel it as though you are living it. Really FEEL the positive emotion.

*See reference section for information about brainwave states.

Practice. Practice. Practice.

We use our imagination every day. More often than not, we are imagining things we do not want. Worrying is a perfect example of this.

It is never a matter of not being able to visualize. It is a matter of practicing and become self-disciplined enough to strategically visualize what we want. *And to limit the amount of negativity we inadvertently visualize.*

One practice I've found particularly helpful is to catch myself if I am worrying or thinking about what I don't want, and intentionally override it with a positive visualization of what I do want. This simple activity can be done through your intention, and does not require that you go into a meditative state or even stop what you are doing. The key is to catch yourself if you go into negative thought forms and intentionally create positive thought forms instead (visualize what you desire, want, or prefer).

The more you practice visualization, the easier it becomes.

Important Points

There are a couple of important points I'd like to make about visualization as a tool to help you achieve your goals. First and foremost, it should always feel good. If, as you are doing your visualization exercise, you feel negative emotion, either stop and work on shifting your mindset (you may be in a state of resistance); or ask yourself whether what you are attempting to create in your life is what you truly desire, it could be that you're going in the wrong direction.

When visualizing what you want to create, see and feel yourself having achieved the desired result. We have a tendency to want to know "how" things are going to happen. But, that is not really our job. Regardless of your spiritually based beliefs, I'm sure you will agree that things have a way of unfolding, often, much differently than we had anticipated. It is my belief and experience that, the Universe (God, Spirit, Source, insert your title) is orchestrating the details. Our job is to clearly define what we want (ideally by using our emotions as a guidance system) and take inspired action.

As you visualize what you want to create/experience, see and feel yourself beyond the actions and/or circumstances that got you there. Jump right into the being, doing or having of what you want. This will keep your subconscious mind from going into doubt and overwhelm over how this will come to pass.

Finally, at the conclusion of your visualization, release any attachment to the outcome. If you have strong faith, this may be easier for you. If you find yourself struggling to let go, you are blocking the manifestation with doubt.

We don't know how things will unfold, nor do we know when they will unfold. However, we can and often do know that they WILL unfold by the way we feel. Practice your visualization and enjoy the process.

Thanks to amazing authors like Dr. David Hawkins and Abraham-Hicks, we know that our emotions can be used like a GPS to guide us to our goals, desires and overall well-being.

When you feel negative emotions you are out of alignment. You are either focusing on what you don't want (instead of what you do want) or you are bumping up against old subconscious conditioning in opposition of your desire.

When you feel positive emotions you are in alignment and on course to achieving-receiving your desired outcome.

Although it is ideal to feel positive most of the time, it is unnatural and unhealthy to repress negative emotions. Be willing to explore your negative emotions, they may have something to show you regarding an old limiting belief.

That said, don't dwell in the negativity. It will only reinforce the old conditioning and block you from being, doing and having what you want.

Chapter 4

Inspired & Aligned Action

Entrepreneurship is in my DNA. Not necessarily by inheritance, but I had the burning desire for that independence early on. Although I won't go into the whole story, I will say that marketing, sales and business have consistently played a role in my life. In retrospect, it is not at all surprising that I became a business coach and consultant. Also not surprising that I would have such an unconventional - borderline metaphysical - approach to marketing and business.

Why inspired action is an important factor in building your lifestyle business.

If you are spiritual, you may resonate with the term inspired action. Even if you are not spiritual, you probably still understand the nature of inspired action. My definition of inspired action is to take action when it feels aligned; more specifically, when you have a powerful urge to create, or to do something, *in this case*, relevant to your business.

We both know that you cannot sit around and wait to do marketing or sales or day to day business operation until you feel inspired. And if you are really stuck, sometimes you have to take action even when you are out of alignment to get things moving and flowing again. BUT the more aligned you are, the more you feel inspired to take certain actions, and the greater the return.

I have taught for a long time, that taking action when you are out of alignment produces less than desirable results. I first stumbled on this fact when I was the sales manager of a retail store in my mid-twenties. One of the owners of the chain was your very stereotypical salesman. All the way down to using the terms *"folks"* and *"bell and whistles"*. Keep in mind, I had done various types of sales prior to taking that position, and had been pretty successful. For me, his approach just felt off; but he was adamant that we do sales *his* way.

Long story short, I tried sales his way and I failed miserably. After eventually letting go of trying to please him, I decided to do sales *my* way; coming from a place of personal integrity – treating my customers with respect – providing honest and factual information – while simultaneously focused on my sales goals. Basically, **I got aligned.** And I became the top sales producer within the company that month, and consistently stayed in the top ranks my three years with the company.

> 66 *Taking action when you are out of alignment produces less than desirable results.*

As an entrepreneur creating your lifestyle business – a business that aligns with who you are and what you really want in life – how you do sales and marketing [the mental and emotional state you are in] is a critical piece of the success puzzle.

From a practical perspective, you must employ marketing methods and a business model that supports your preferences.

When it comes to taking any actions in your business, whether it is sales, marketing, delivering your product or service, or communicating with employees... do your best be in alignment. It will always produce better results. And when it comes to important projects, alignment often results in inspired action which is behind virtually every significant success.

Chapter 5

Letting Go of What Does Not Serve You

Part of this mindset, marketing and making of your lifestyle business is letting go of what no longer serves you, what no longer fits with who you have become and how you live your life. Just like you would not wear the same jeans you wore when you were 16 years old (I know my style and body have changed since then), there are certain things you had been doing in your life and business that don't support the person you want to be.

What are some of the things you have been doing in your life or business that you know are not in alignment with what you truly want?

You'll notice that I am asking you to be very honest with yourself again. This is important, because if you say you want something, but you are not willing to do what it takes, then you are not really committed. You have not made the decision yet.

I would like to use an analogy here – a little NLP (Neuro-Linguistic Programing). Let's pretend we know a woman who is in an unhappy relationship. She knows she wants to be in a new relationship with a different man who makes her feel loved and appreciated. She believes she is ready for this new relationship, so she visits on a dating website and creates a profile to meet the perfect new partner. She even meets someone who appears to be exactly what she wants... but, there is a problem. She is still in a relationship with the man who makes her unhappy.

Assuming we are on the same page about this woman's desire for a monogamous relationship, we know she needs to leave the existing relationship before she can have what she really wants with a new partner. If she doesn't let go of the old relationship, she cannot have what she really desires. Even if she were to enter into a new relationship while staying in the old relationship, she would not be as happy as she wants to be because she is still holding onto the unhappy relationship.

Our friend needs to let go and make room in her life for what she wants. Like her, you might have taken all the right steps to have what you want, but have been holding onto something that is contributing to your unhappiness.

Be aware of what you have been tolerating in your life or business. What must change in order to make room in your life for what you want? What can you let go of that no longer serves you?

Blueprint for Your Lifestyle Business

It is time to make some changes. You have identified what you *really* want. You have identified some things that no longer serve you (things to let go of – mentally, emotionally, and in your current business). Now it is time to create the plan to shift from your previous lifestyle and business, into your chosen lifestyle and business. Are you ready?

Assessment

In my business, before brining on a new client, I do an assessment of their current business, marketing and mindset. This serves a variety of purposes. On the one hand, I need this information to better serve them. <u>And</u> this assessment helps me clearly determine whether they are ready for the changes they say they want.

I encourage you to treat this assessment with the same respect. On the one hand, this information will help you create a plan based on Where You Are and Where You Want to Be. Similar to creating a plan for a cross country trip, you need to know the destination and the directions.

Additionally, if you are honest with yourself, you will be able to clearly determine whether you are ready for the changes you say you want. Two telltale signs you are not ready are 1) Procrastination and Excuses 2) Resistance which could be in the form of overwhelm, stress, physical ailments, or manifesting unexpected dramatic and demanding issues.

Assessment Questions for Implementing Your Blueprint:

o   Can you clearly define and articulate what you really want?

Write it down in a notebook. Rewrite it until it feels right if necessary. If you are really honest with yourself, you should feel good (aligned) with your response. If it doesn't feel right, go through the exercise in Chapter 1. Then revisit this activity.

o   What are the obstacles that have been in the way of you having what you really want?

o   What can you do to solve, or overcome, these obstacles? If you don't know, who can help you?

o   Are you willing to do what is necessary to resolve the obstacles-challenges which have held you back in the past?

Rate yourself on the following 1-10 scale for each obstacle: 0 = I am NOT willing to change. 10 = No one could possibly stop me from changing.

o   What skills do you need to develop, tasks need to be delegated, team members or experts need to be hired, or new strategies need to be implemented to achieve the level of success and quality of life you desire?

Break each of these down and set realistic goals for achieving each one.

Chapter 7

The "Keys" to Your Lifestyle Business

You are clear about what you want, and what you need to do to create it. Before you take massive action on your blueprint, it is important to address the key elements of your ideal "lifestyle business".

For instance, do you want more autonomy? More control over your time? Perhaps, in the past, you made your cell phone number available to clients, customers, vendors, etc. Moving forward, you may want to hire an assistant to screen your calls and schedule appointments.

Or perhaps you want your clients to travel to you for appointments instead of you traveling to them, it may be time to review your existing procedures and adjust them accordingly.

As you determine how you want your business and life to flow, you must build these lifestyle changes into your business.

Identifying your key elements:

Do you need to raise your prices to accommodate the lifestyle changes you want?

If you want more free time, then you may have to increase your fees and work with fewer clients. Or perhaps you need to build a leveraged income model, like offering group programs which allow you to help more people within the same amount of time.

Consider:

- How many hours would you like to work each week?

- What is your annual income goal?

Based on the hours you want to work and your income goals are you on track for what you want? If not, what needs to change to be on track?

Income Formula

Annual Income Goal =

Divide by 52 for weekly income necessary to achieve your goal.

Weekly Income Goal =

Ideal Hours per Week =

Divide Hours into Weekly Income to determine the hourly rate you must average to achieve your goal.

Average Hourly Rate =

What other changes would you like to make in your business and life?

- Do you want to work from home?

- Would you like to start speaking or consulting?

- Do you want to create passive income streams?

Take some time to identify how your lifestyle business operates. What other key elements must be built into your business, marketing and sales strategies to accommodate your goals?

Chapter 8

Marketing Your Lifestyle Business

Everyone's version of a lifestyle business is different; therefore, your marketing strategy will be unique. However, the average successful entrepreneur typically utilizes a handful of highly effective methods to grow and sustain their ideal business. I won't spend too much time on the details of each strategy or tactic; the intention of this chapter is to help you clarify what marketing strategies are *best for you* to implement.

Caveat: There are many experts who teach specific techniques. I do not profess to be an expert at every marketing tactic I suggest, recommend, and reference or even use for that matter. That being said, I have been marketing online since 2002, so I have been around long enough to know a few things. Additionally, I am an avid marketing student, especially of direct response marketing. My suggestions are based on success in my business, as well for the clients I have consulted over the past few years.

Overview of marketing strategies

Here I will quickly reference several effective (when correctly implemented) marketing methods. Ideally you will become proficient at the ones you choose to make a part of your overall marketing strategy. Be mindful of whether they are a good fit for you and your ideal lifestyle business.

Marketing Platforms:

Professional Speaking (Keynotes, Speak to Sell Opportunities)

Direct Mail (Strategic Mailing Campaigns)

Online Marketing (Lead Generation Techniques, Sales Pages)

Media Appearances (TV, Radio Interviews, Write Ups)

Credibility and Leverage Marketing Strategies:

Authorship (Book, Articles in Prestigious Publications)

Strategic Partnerships (Joint Ventures, Win-Win Cooperation)

Sponsorships (Specifically Events with Your Ideal Customers)

Referral Strategies (Strategic Referral System)

Now, let's break each of these down...

Professional Speaking

Professional Speaking is not everyone's cup of tea. If the thought of speaking in front of hundreds or thousands of people makes you queasy, then this is not ideal for your lifestyle business marketing model. However, if you love teaching, motivating and inspiring others and/or like to be the center of attention, than this is a powerful marketing tool when done correctly.

The two primary categories of professional speaking include Keynote Presentations and Speak to Sell Opportunities. A Keynote is when you get paid to present your information. For the average speaker, they may charge anywhere from $2,500 - $10,000+ depending on experience and demand.

The other way speaking can work to your advantage is Speak to Sell Opportunities. In this instance, you may or may not get paid a speaking fee; however, you can pitch your product or service during or after your presentation. I highly encourage you to seek out additional training in this area; it is a skill that is not intuitive for most people.

Clearly, speaking is advantageous with regard to reaching a larger audience, especially if you are speaking in front of the right group of people. It also builds credibility and can enhance name recognition.

Direct Mail

Direct mail is usually underutilized or used ineffectively. When used strategically, it can be a powerful marketing tool. As a student of Dan Kennedy (who I highly recommend you learn from if you are not already) I've learned a great deal about how to create effective direct mail campaigns.

Mail can be used to generate highly qualified prospects; for instance, mailing a promotional piece offering your free lead magnet*. Then collecting their information and entering them into your sales funnel. Or mail can be used to nurture and convert prospects into customers, clients or patients.

Where a lot of businesses fail with direct mail is a lack of solid marketing strategy. A one shot mailing to an untargeted list is like flushing money down the toilet. But, a series of well-crafted mailings to your ideal prospects can be extremely profitable.

* Lead Magnet: You offer something valuable for free in exchange for the prospects contact information and permission to contact them either by email, mail and/or phone.

Online Marketing

This is a big area. I have been marketing online for many years and it has changed a lot during that time. I remember when the "best" traffic generating tactics were writing articles and publishing them in online article directories, and/or getting back links on as many other websites as possible. And it worked!

Now there are so many ways to market online it can be overwhelming. Consumers are overloaded as well. Not only are they desensitized to advertising messages, they don't trust anyone.

Keep in mind, this area of marketing is always changing. So I highly recommend you practice discernment before investing in the latest social media course or pay thousands of dollars for SEO. While I am not saying these things are not valuable, I am saying that may well intending entrepreneurs have lost a lot of money very quickly for little to nothing in return.

On a more positive note; online marketing can be both effective and provide tremendous leverage. Today, you **need** an online presence to be taken seriously. And with the right online presence and strategic marketing strategy you have abundantly more freedom and ability to create a lifestyle business.

Some key benefits to consider:

- ✓ The internet eliminates demographic and time constraints.

- ✓ Marketing can be done fairly affordably compared to other advertising mediums.

- ✓ The ability to reach highly targeted prospects is consistently becoming easier and more effective.

I have personally had a great deal of success in business by marketing online. In fact, in December 2012 "I let go" of my local office and went completely virtual. I was able to do that because of modern technology and online marketing.

As of the writing of this book, video marketing is very popular. I have personally attracted a significant amount of business through YouTube videos.

Other effective online marketing strategies include PPC (Pay-Per-Click) and social media marketing. Caveat: These techniques can be expensive. Or worse, expensive and not yield results. I recommend hiring a professional to assist you with your campaigns. And/or invest time in learning the fundamentals.

Media Appearances

Media appearances can be a powerful business growth strategy. In fact, I launched my hypnotherapy practice and filled it for about two months from just one write up in the local paper. A second write up in a smaller local publication yielded another rush of new clients.

If you are featured as an expert (or simply a guest) on a well-respected Radio Show, TV, magazine or newspaper, it can give you massive exposure and create immediate credibility. A good PR campaign with lots of exposure and an effective marketing system to capture and nurture leads can help you grow your business fast.

Regardless of how sophisticated your clients or customers are the average person cannot help but associate credibility with media appearances and article write ups. Position yourself as an expert in your field, develop a relevant hook that grabs the media's attention, and take advantage of all the free publicity you can get.

One of the most effective ways to get on radio or TV is to author a book, seguing perfectly into our next section.

Authorship

From a marketing perspective, writing a book is a valuable marketing tool. While not a small task, it can provide a lot of credibility, as well as opportunities.

I stated in the media appearance section, a book is one of the most effective ways for a non-celebrity to get free media exposure. I used my first book to get dozens of media opportunities. A book can also be used as a marketing tool through book launch campaigns, handed out to prospective clients like a glorified business card, or as a gift in giveaways or other promotional opportunities.

Although a book is not the only mode of gaining credibility as a trusted authority, it is one I highly recommend. That being said, writing for a prestigious magazine, blog or newspaper can also help.

Strategic Partnerships

Growing a successful business requires the right mindset, an investment of time, and usually money. Although you can create a great deal of success on your own, leveraging the power of people and partnerships is definitely a smart business decision.

While it is obvious to many entrepreneurs that you can exponentially increase your reach by forming strategic alliances with other powerful people in complementary markets, I've found that many of my clients, regardless of the size of their business, are under-utilizing this strategy.

If you are not currently implementing strategic partnerships, I highly recommend you give it some serious consideration. Who could you connect with to form a win-win business relationship? What do you have that they could benefit from, and vise versa?

Every business is different; you may need to think outside the box. Come up with a few angles that are really appealing, and strategically choose which approach you will use based on the prospective partner. One example that I've used over the years is offering to interview colleagues on my podcast. It gives them additional exposure and helps them to build credibility as an expert on their respective topic. It is a great door opener for me to discuss how we can mutually benefit from working together on a project, or some type of endorsement to the other's network of clients, customers, followers, etc.

Sponsorships

There are different ways to benefiting from sponsorships. You can be a sponsor at events, or sponsor gifts for event giveaways. Both of these will give your business additional exposure to varying degrees. I've had a great deal of success getting new clients by sponsoring gift certificates for local Chamber of Commerce events, radio station events, and other types of high exposure opportunities.

Especially popular in the coaching industry is "sponsoring" a booth at a conference or high end training event. More often than not this will cost you a few thousand dollars, so preparation is key to making it worth your time and money. That being said, you can cherry pick which events to sponsor based on where your ideal clients and customers will be. These events naturally put people into a buying mode, and if you can stand out from the crowd, it can be extremely lucrative.

Referral Strategies

There are lots of statistics on how profoundly valuable referrals are. If you have been in business for any length of time, then you probably know that referrals are some of the easiest sales. I am not going to go into why referrals are great… I will assume you already know. However, it is worth mentioning that there are ways that you can increase the amount of referrals you get. In fact, I believe almost any type of business can incorporate a referral system into their existing business model. If you happen to be in an industry that regulates against certain practices, then you need to get creative about how you language *and reward* your referral offer.

One of the most effective times to ask for a referral (or indirectly present your referral offer) is directly after your client or customer had a great experience. This will vary from business to business.

As a coach, I've found that the best time is at the end of a really great session (*well… they are all great* ;-) … Usually, it is the first or second session when they express how grateful they are for the results they are getting.

If you are selling a product, the opportune time is likely upon delivery or shortly after.

Ideally, you want to present the offer when they are most excited about your product or service. And sweeten the deal by offering something you know they would love to have; for instance, a bonus session for the referral of a new client.

For your referral system to work, you have to offer something that they will LOVE. There needs to be real incentive because most people have internal resistance to making a referral. It also needs to be financially smart for you. If you know that the lifetime value of a customer or client is $1,000. Then you can pretty comfortably reward your referring customer a $50 gift card. Or perhaps better yet, a $150 gift certificate to use towards their next big purchase with you.

Once you are clear on what the perfect referral reward is, now you must be consistent with offering it to your clients or customers. If you can find a way to automate it, or make it a part of your overall strategy/approach, it will greatly increase the amount of referral business you get.

Closing Thoughts

We really just scratched the surface with regard to marketing. The fact is, there is no shortage of 'how-to' training available. And there is no shortage of strategies or tactics that can work well for you. Furthermore, if you are already somewhat established, then much of this is old news anyway. So my closing thought is this…

When you are passionate about your business, the rest tends to fall into place. If you are continuously resisting certain aspects of your business, whether it is a marketing approach, a type of client you can't stand, a process that seems to suck the life out of you, or anything else for that matter, then it is time for some self-honesty and recalibrating.

Life is not meant to be a continuous struggle. Most of us have been taught that. But, not only is it not true, it is not serving you or anyone else. Not your family, friends, clients, customers, employees… not anyone. Period. And when you come to realize that very little is worth being miserable, including money, you will also realize that it is time to approach life and business differently. This little book is intended to be a reminder. Because on some level you already knew that things could be… should be… different. Now is a good time to choose to do things differently.

In the words of Abraham-Hicks, "You can't get it wrong and you can't get it done." Life is really just one course correction after the next. So take it easy on yourself. Spend more time doing things that feel good and are aligned with you.

Chapter 9

The Journey of the Entrepreneur...

By Guest Author: Michael E. Schmidlen

"Go to college, study hard, find a good job, get married, buy a house, and have kids." - Since the end of World War II, the de-facto definition of the traditional "American Dream"

This advice has been uttered daily in homes all across America for generations. I was one of those who also heard this advice from my parents, peers and teachers... They all had the best of intentions in mind...

And I too lived tried to live this life right out of high school and found a warehouse job with a big American corporation (I had decided NOT to go the college route for many reasons). I was on a broken down rocket ship to middle management baby. I was being lulled to sleep with a steady paycheck, the illusion of "safety & security" of working for a large company, and the ephemeral promise of a "comfortable" retirement.

I played along for over 9 years and I finally got to a point where something just didn't seem quite right for me anymore. I knew there was more to life than merely "existing" and the work I was doing and getting paid peanuts for was no longer satisfying and was something I knew I could do on my own and probably make a lot more money doing it that way, while also having the ability to control my own destiny. My personal reality was that I was too entrepreneurial to work in a large, structured corporate environment.

If you were to check into the backgrounds of the 50 richest people in the world, I can promise you that the list is littered with entrepreneurs who also went against conventional thinking and wisdom, who either dropped out of school, or started with ZERO schooling, and went on to achieve massive business success.

It was in their heart and they knew exactly what they wanted to do, they most likely didn't have the blueprint to get there, but they still took the risk and massive action and achieved success despite the "odds" against them.

I was determined to follow this path… not the conventional one that everyone else was on.

So as my wife was mere months away from giving birth to our first child, I took the leap and branched out on my own. We were scared to death, but I had the support of my wife and a few others and jumped off the cliff and have never looked back.

For over 25 years, I have had the very good fortune of being on my own personal entrepreneurial journey. As you would expect, based on my longevity, there have been many more good times than bad times, but make no mistake about it, there have been plenty of both!

I've also learned many business and life lessons along the way and if I've proven anything to myself, it's that I'm gratefully "unemployable". By that I mean that while I've learned "Never to say Never", it would be almost impossible for me to go to work for someone else at this stage of my life and career.

Even when things have gone really bad, I never once thought that the "solution" was to go to work for someone else. Being an entrepreneur is certainly NOT for everyone, as there's a very good reason (many actually!) why we can't all be leaders, and need to have some followers as part of the team.

While I obviously can't share all of the many lessons that I've learned, I can share the three most significant areas that have personally served me very well. If I were to attempt to distill down what I've learned, or to offer you a blueprint to entrepreneurial success for those just getting started, this would be my starting advice.

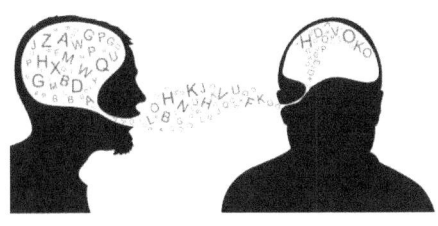

WHO do YOU listen to???

The first of these areas is the distillation of the enormous amount information that is now available to all of us… there are no excuses when it comes to finding information or ideas of how to be a successful entrepreneur or to live a better life.

As we continue on the journey, one of the most important questions that we all need to figure out is: "Who do YOU listen to"? I first heard this expression a couple of years ago and the message still remains very valid.

One thing to keep in mind when it comes to information on any subject is that the person providing the information is speaking from personal experience in most cases. Your experiences are going to be different obviously.

In the information age we have the ability to instantly research virtually any subject under the sun, and receive 10's, hundred's, thousands and even millions of potential sources of information.

How do you really know who to listen to? Who to trust to provide you with accurate, timely & relevant information? What "filters" do you use?

While I'm not suggesting that you don't listen to the "guru's" of the world, I would caution that you do so carefully, and question what their motivation(s) may be with the advice they are offering to you.

Also, it's important for you to decide if their message and personality are aligned with your values & beliefs. Does their message resonate with you? Or does it cause you to pause and give it a second, or more thought(s)?

Ultimately you will learn that you need to listen to yourself…

Because the thoughts that you think, the words that you use, what and how you feel, as well as the actions that you take, or don't take, are a much better reflection of your subconscious beliefs than any external input you can ever receive.

It has been my experience that the information and guidance I am seeking is usually found within me. Often I have just felt that I needed external validation from someone else. Of course you will always find tidbits of information that you didn't know before that will help you streamline your business or life, but the major decisions and life altering paths that you choose must come from YOU and not someone else.

This leads us to the second significant area that I'd like to address.

In case you didn't know it – the Self-Development/Self-Improvement Industry is not just about feeling good. According to Wikipedia and Psychology Today, this is a more than $11 Billion dollar industry – and growing more every successive year.

It took me quite a bit of time in my career to figure out that while I had invested substantially in my technical knowledge since very early in my career, I had not invested in the most important education subject: ME!

For me, these personal investments have certainly paid the best dividends!

"Self-Help" or "Shelf-Help"?

"An investment in knowledge pays the best interest"
- Benjamin Franklin

In this age of short attention spans, information overload and instant gratification, we're ALL looking for the "EASY" button; to change our habits, to improve our lives, to add to our knowledge and expertise, to lose weight or to find our soul mate.

The simple truth is that there ISN'T one.

All of these things are possible, and NOT overly difficult or complicated to achieve, but they don't happen by "magic", or by pressing a simple button. What they DO require is focused and determined effort and action on our parts.

It helps to have a clear understanding of the "WHY" in what we want/need to learn, so that we can realistically decide and evaluate if a program is going to provide that answer, or at least send us down the correct path towards our ultimate goal(s).

I have rightly been described as being an "information sponge" and have also been a big proponent of investing in one's personal self-education, as well as furthering your professional education & skills.

I have received much benefit from this practice, but I've also experienced just as many disappointments in my efforts and substantial expenditures, of both time and money. This has occurred mostly when I've tried to seek in others, or their products, what I wanted to see in them, as opposed to what was actually there or the benefit(s) they would realistically provide to me.

This also supports "Who Are You Listening To". I wanted someone else to show me how to do it... The easy button if you will. Hint: There is no easy button, and anybody selling one is lying.

I was recently on my first call with my new personal business coach, something I would advise all of you to do as quickly as possible, which is get a coach. During our conversation, we were discussing my past efforts and "rather impressive" collection of self-improvement and self-development books,

DVD's and programs, when he used a term that I'd never heard before: "Shelf-Help", to describe our propensity to buy self-improvement or self-development books and/or products, that we do so with the best of intentions, but that we NEVER use, instead allowing them to collect dust on the shelf.

I'm certainly "GUILTY" of this behavior, as my family will readily attest. The problem with this type of behavior, while it may be well-meaning & good intentioned, is that it can cause the following negative outcomes:

> 1)   It can provide you with a false sense of security. Thinking that just having the course or book instantly makes you a better business man.

> 2)   It can cause you to feel overwhelmed and more confused. I would sometimes shutdown or grow irritable when I would start trying to learn something new. There is so much to learn and implement. I use this metaphor before I get started on a new course or book: "How do you eat and elephant? One bite at a time."

> 3)   It can also cause you to become more indecisive. You're not sure the best path or course to take... the information is pulling you in a different direction then you started out on.

> 4)   It can cause you to always be chasing the next "magic pill", or solution, and never focusing on finishing

and MASTERING the program(s) that you already own (a perpetual dog chasing his tail).

5)   It can cost you a lot of time, which isn't replaceable, and a lot of money, which is.

In the end, I would still make all of the personal investments that I've made in the past, and will continue to so invest in the future, but I will do so with the understanding and knowledge that the mere act of purchase does not constitute an "education." Action is ALWAYS necessary for growth.

My suggestion to you is to finish and master one program at a time, before you're distracted by the next flashy, wiz-bang, shiny object that's sure to come along. Make it a part of your daily routine and set aside an hour or two a day and go through the book, or course that you purchased and put the information/knowledge/idea into action.

The first two points are "tools", and they set the table for the feast that is about to take place. This final section deals with actionable daily mindsets that I have used, and continue to use to take my life and business to the next level.

"Without continual growth and progress, such words as improvement, achievement, and success have no meaning."
- Benjamin Franklin

The 10 Pillars of Success

I have enjoyed a healthy dose of both success & failure over the 30+ years I have been in the business world and I will share with you that success is certainly more "fun", and it definitely pays better too! While I will concede that there are MANY different pillars of success, these are my personal top 10 favorites.

1. ACTION: You MUST take focused action on a DAILY basis towards your dreams and goals or you highly likely WON'T achieve them. The most successful people out there are the ones who have embraced these ideas and are DOING something to build their businesses. Taking targeted/focused action and making changes can be uncomfortable at first, but stick with it and watch what can happen!

TIP: Establish a goals checklist, a personal "roadmap" so that you can track your step-by-step journey to success!

2. ATTITUDE: As Henry Ford once famously said: "If you believe you can do a thing or you can't do a thing, you're right." It is YOUR attitude that will either unlock or bolt shut the door to success!!! Dare to dream (and achieve) GREAT things, and then go make it happen! The ONLY difference between those who thrive and those who flounder is in their heads, successful people DECIDE to succeed! What are YOU going to decide to do???

TIP: Your attitude is a choice that you make; you can choose to be positive, or you can be negative, the choice is yours alone to make!

3. DEDICATION: The reality of today's business climate is that EVERYONE has to "do more with less", working long days & weeks are now the new "normal", and dedication to one's profession is NO longer "optional". This ISN'T saying that you can't strive for "work-life" balance, but understand it's NOT something that you can any longer take lightly.

TIP: I truly believe that you MUST have priorities, and taking responsibility & care of one's family (if you have one), should be at the TOP of your list. The BEST way to do that is to excel at your job, profession or business.

4. FOCUS: By being focused on your goals, you can avoid the trap of "shiny object syndrome", the single biggest distraction that most entrepreneurs face. Find the balance between "tunnel vision" (being TOO focused) and being ALL over the place (being completely unfocused) in your thinking and actions.

A trick that has helped me: Set a time limit for using social media and e-mail.

5. HABITS: Successful people have arrived at their success by establishing & maintaining the necessary habits to enable them to achieve their goals. There are obviously "good habits" and "bad habits". There is NO hard & fast list of good habits, but I would suggest that these are 8 of the key habits to develop and nurture for long-term success:

a. Start your day, each & every day, off on the right foot.

b. Take regular breaks during the day. "ME" time (Meditation, listening to soothing music, walking, etc.) is VERY important to both your mental & emotional health.

c. Try to consistently eat well. Maintain the temple. Not only does it make you feel better, but it's better for you too.

d. Utilize technology. Control it, or it WILL control you. It's a tool, and like any other it must be properly maintained to maximize its effectiveness.

e. Maintain a flexible daily "To Do" list. Take care of your most profitable & important tasks first.

f. Strive to balance your workload. Delegate those tasks that you struggle with and focus on the things that you excel at.

g. Understand that perfection DOESN'T exist, so put the desire to be "perfect" in its proper place!

h. Learn how to say "NO". Your time is a finite resource, treat it like gold!

TIP: Do what works best for you! I'm constantly working on these to refine them for myself.

6. HARD WORK: The United States, in spite of ALL of its faults, is still regarded around the world as the BEST place to start with absolutely nothing, and based solely on your willingness to engage in hard work, have passion about what you're doing, perseverance and patience in achieving your goals, you can ACHIEVE almost anything. It truly is the land of opportunity. Nowhere else have so many stories been written about "rags to riches" and they happen here EVERY day. NO place on Earth is the equal of the U.S. when it comes to honoring and rewarding hard work.

Tip: Reward yourself for achieving goals & milestones, you've earned it!

7. PASSION: Passion is the first thing you think about when you wake up in the morning and the last thing you think about before you go to bed at night. It can feel like an addiction, and if someone were to tell you to stop, it would be difficult, if not impossible for you to give it up. Those who have uncovered their passion feel compelled to pursue it, whether or not they are getting paid to do it. You MUST give your passion fuel and room to grow. Your passion has the need to expand, and the surest way to do that is to share it with others.

TIP: Strive to spend more time with others who share your passion and spend less time with those who do not.

8. PATIENCE, PERSEVERANCE & PERSISTENCE: The 3 legged stool of long-term success.

> "Failure is only the opportunity to begin again, only this time more wisely." – Henry Ford

The road to success is often paved with failure – and failure can be a very expensive education, but it's ultimately worth it!

> "Our greatest weakness lies in giving up. The most certain way to succeed is always to try just one more time" – Thomas A. Edison

TIP: While it can & likely will be difficult at times, long-term success requires patience and a willingness to endure the tough times knowing that you can pull through them and emerge better for the experience.

9. PLANNING: "Success is a journey, NOT a destination" - Make conscious choices & decisions instead of dwelling on what you "should" be doing. This will enable you to reach your goals quicker and help you to ensure your path to success.

TIP: Set-up a list of written goals and objectives, read them daily, keep track of one's you've achieved and add new ones.

10. VISION, WISDOM: Understand that no matter how "smart" you actually are (or think that you are), you CANNOT predict the future. There's a HUGE difference between vision and prognostication; having vision is a "good thing", in that it allows you to survey the business landscape and try to determine what direction things are headed, while prognostication typically sets you up to become ridiculed, marginalized or ruins your reputation and credibility.

TIP: I humbly suggest that you use tools, such as a Vision Board, to help keep you focused on your personal goals & dreams. It serves as a constant reminder and is a visual representation of WHAT you want. It can include pictures, words or other items which have significance to you & your dreams.

I've personally used these three "tools" with great success over the course of my career, and will continue to utilize them each and every day. These are my cornerstones.

I would be remiss if I didn't also share with you some of my most recent adventures. While I have fortunately enjoyed many great successes and a couple of failures too, over the course of my career as I've previously noted, I became disillusioned with my "day job" starting in mid-2010 through much of 2011. I was trying to figure out what was going to be the next "big thing" for me, another career transition so-to-speak, and because I had successfully chosen a technology trend in 2003 that ultimately led me to millions of dollars of business, I was confident that I could do it again. However, there was one "little" problem that I had to contend with. I wasn't quite certain how I'd gotten to the mountain top, and choosing a path back up has proven to be very difficult for me personally & professionally. (I'm still searching!).

During this time period, I was introduced to the CEO of a mobile software start-up company by a mutual friend. While I didn't have any previous experience selling software, I had been an early adopter of mobile technology (I have had a mobile phone since 1985) and while I didn't completely understand their technology, I readily recognized the significance of what they had accomplished. I became emotionally attached to the idea of the promise that the technology had, which clearly clouded my judgment, and as a result I overlooked obvious warning signs that were apparent to literally everyone I introduced this individual to, including my wife. I would ultimately pay a very heavy price for this decision. This lapse in judgment cost me over 3 years of my life, and tied-up $260,000.00 in a company with no assets or revenue, while ignoring the fact that the CEO I had invested with and in, had no idea how to take this potential and turn it into a profit. I virtually ignored my own company during this time as I completely threw myself into trying to help them take their product to market, naively hoping that I might be able to parlay a substantial personal financial investment and my time and connections into my "winning lottery ticket".

I came back to these three fundamental mindset hacks and began the journey to recoup my investment and leave this toxic "opportunity" behind. I learned a valuable life lesson with this experience and fortunately was financially made "whole" about a year ago now.

While I could have very easily allowed this bad experience to sour me on outside investment opportunities, I instead decided to learn from the experience and have it make me better, instead of bitter. Opportunities are always around us, if we choose to see them or seek them out.

The next time an opportunity presented itself, which was last fall, I did my due diligence homework and didn't allow the dream of a potential big payday (because we ALL know that you CAN'T spend "potential") cloud the harsh reality of the difficulty of making a profit on technological innovation. Without these three tools and past experiences, I may well have jumped back into another "bad" investment, as opposed to going through my mental checklist and listening to my heart and gut. This time, I made a MUCH smarter decision and am on the verge of benefitting from my vision and the vision of my partners. The "easy" part is over (the 24 months of development); now the "hard" part begins: taking it to market & monetizing it! I am excited about the possibilities that this investment offers me, and the potential for a very sizable return that exists if we succeed.

My hope for you all is that you too will utilize these tools, or your own set, with great success…

Michael E. Schmidlen is a serial solo entrepreneur who has successfully run his multimillion dollar, home-based business for over 20 years. Michael is currently working on finishing his first book, "THE Underwear Entrepreneur" The Definitive Guide To Working From Home, where he shares his many business experiences and unique stories. The book is designed to be a blueprint for other small business owners, would-be entrepreneurs and start-ups to beat the overwhelming odds to create a successful, thriving small business model. He is also currently publishing two new business-themed magazines: CRUSHING IT Magazine and UNDERWEAR ENTREPRENEUR Magazine, in addition to running his business.

http://www.crushingitmag.com

http://www.advanceddatacomm.com

http://www.underwearentrepreneur.com

Chapter 11

Do Less and Accomplish More

From the book "Finding Purpose and Joy, It's a Journey"
by Guest Author Roger Laidig

"The best use of our time is spent in preventing future crises."

Early in my management career at Laidig, Inc., at Christmas one of the employees that were under my supervision gave me a small trophy of a fireman with a plate that said "Fire Chief of the Year". While I believe he meant it to be a compliment based on how busy I was, it made me think. If I was a champion fire fighter, something must be wrong with my leadership abilities. The best leaders prevent crises instead of fighting them.

What is the best use of our time could also be known as good time management. Time management is the act or process of planning and exercising conscious control over the amount of time spent on specific activities, especially to increase effectiveness, efficiency or productivity. There are an abundance of books, classes, workshops, day-planners, and seminars on time management, which teach individuals and corporations how to be more organized and more productive. Time management has become crucial in recent years thanks to the 24/7, busy world in which we live.

PRIORITIES

As you begin thinking about the best use of your time, it's probably a good time to clearly identify your priorities based on where you hope to end up in the future. Here is one way of doing that.

Remember the wagon wheels from the old 'wild west' movies? Now picture each spoke of the wheel as an aspect of your life. For purpose of this example, each spoke represents a different aspect...

- Spiritual well-being

- Family

- Work and financial well-being

- Physical well-being

- Emotional well-being

These spokes are simply suggestions that seem to be common for a lot of people. If they are not quite on the mark for you, rename them to fit your life.

If you are living a balanced life by paying attention to each facet of your life, the wagon travels smoothly down the road. But if your life gets out-of-whack and you're spending a lot more time in some facets while neglecting others, what happens? The road of life becomes quite bumpy and perhaps rocky at best. So as you consider big picture time management, perhaps it would be a good idea to think about ALL aspects of your life and not just work at whichever you tend to favor.

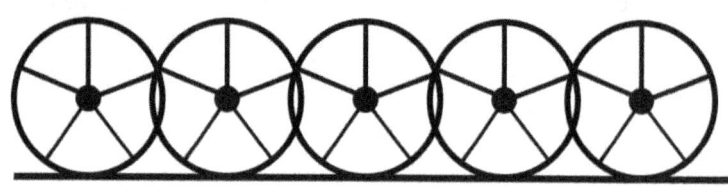

A balanced life runs smoothly down the road.

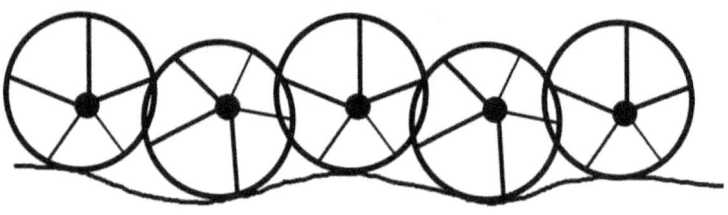

An unbalanced life leads to a chaotic and bumpy road.

FOUR QUADRANTS

Over the years, I've learned about and used various time management systems but as of this time, one has risen above the rest for me. Perhaps you will find it to be of value also. It is the 'Four Quadrants' method that was introduced to me by Stephen Covey in his book, "7 Habits of Highly Effective People."

	Urgent	Non-Urgent
Important	1	2
Non-Important	3	4

In this illustration,

- Q1 (Quadrant 1) represents activities that you spend time on that are both urgent and important

- Q2, activities that are not urgent but important

- Q3, activities that seem urgent but not important

- Q4, activities that are neither urgent or important

This method has been around several years so you may well be familiar with it. If that's the case, this can serve as a way to dust it off and think about how you are using your time . . . a refresher. If this is the first time that you've seen it, hopefully it will give you a new perspective on your use of time.

Here are some questions to ponder...

- What are examples of activities for each quadrant?

- In which quadrant do you think most people spend their time?

- In which quadrant do you spend most of your time?

- Which quadrant would be the best place to use more time?

- How can you find more time to spend in that quadrant?

Quadrant 1 – Activities that are Important and Urgent

Q1 is the quadrant of CRISIS. This quadrant is where most people unwittingly spend a lot of their time. Q1 may be referred to as the quadrant of necessity and contains the tasks that are urgent and important. These are the tasks you have to do or else you will face negative consequences. Usually these are deadline driven and/or time sensitive. On a daily basis, it is inevitable that you will do tasks that fall in Q1. The key is to being able to manage these.

Q1 tasks include:

- Medical emergencies

- Filing your taxes

- Last minute changes

- Tasks that have deadlines

If you feel like you are **firefighting** most of your days, it is a sign that you are spending too much time in this quadrant. You are just doing the things that are crisis oriented. The question is, "How can I get out of this rat race? Hint, you want to shift investing more time in long-term solutions (see Q2). When I was given the "Fire Chief of the Year" trophy, I was obviously spending far too much time in this quadrant.

Quadrant 2 – Important and Not Urgent

Q2 is the quadrant of PREVENTION. This is THE quadrant where you want to invest most of your time. You may question this because these tasks are not urgent. While that's true, they are all about prevention of future crisis. Q2 tasks should be designed to prevent potential Q1 tasks from ever happening. Tasks in Q2 are in direct alignment with your vision and lead you to where you desire to be down the road. They are things you want to achieve in the long run. Here are a few examples of quadrant two tasks:

- Designing and implementing systems to prevent future crisis at work and home. This is what I needed to do in order to do less firefighting at work.

- Include time for all aspects of your 'wagon wheel' of life

- Scheduling some quiet time to refresh your spiritual and emotional well-being

- Spending time with your family and friends

- Exercising

- Developing and following a budget

- Taking classes outside your job to advance your career

Everyone's goals and dreams are different. What might be a Q2 task for me, might not be for you. Also, do you see that the tasks are non-urgent? This might seem counterintuitive at first. A lot of times we associate things that have a sense of urgency as important, but that is not the case. Your desires and dreams are not running away; they will be right where they are now and there is no urgency to achieving them within a specified timeline. Anything that benefits you in the long run could be considered in Q2.

Quadrant 3 – Not important and Urgent

Q3 is the quadrant of DECEPTION. People often confuse these as being important tasks while in fact they are not. Or people think the task is urgent but it really is not (and thus should belong in Q4).

A common occurrence of mistaking something as important is when someone is asking you to do something that does not directly help you achieve your goals. The key here is being able to say "no" to these people.

An example of this at home came early in our marriage when I played on a softball team with co-workers and friends. That event in and of itself wasn't a problem. The problem was that when the games were over, I allowed my friends to convince me that it was really important to go out for some drinks and fellowship. And because this didn't rate very high on Susan's list, this activity then moved to Q1, a crisis.

Examples of mistaking something as urgent, while they are not, are often sources of distraction. For example,

- Doing things that other people tell you are urgent but they really aren't

- Doing easy things rather than what needs to be done.

- Picking up the phone while you are working

- Constantly checking your email inbox and responding right away.

- Constantly checking Facebook updates

- Continually checking your phone for text messages

Quadrant 4 – Not important and Not Urgent

Q4 is the quadrant of WASTED TIME. It contains the tasks you want to avoid as much as possible. These are time wasters that you want to eliminate. If you could identify all your Q4 tasks and eliminate most of them, you would free up a lot of time you could otherwise invest in quadrant two tasks.

Some examples include doing these things in <u>excess</u>:

- Playing video games

- Watching reruns of your favorite TV shows

- Following the news

- Checking your social media

- Most things that you do in excess

The caveat is that this quadrant can be mistaken as something that shouldn't be part of life, but that is not true. It is really important to have a **balanced life between work and your personal life**. You need downtime to not get burnt out and that is where Q2 comes into the picture. The challenge is you allocate most of your time to Q2, with just enough of time spent in Q4 to get by.

The real key to effective time management using the Four Quadrants is continually evaluating time that you are spending in Q3 and Q4 and shifting that time to invest it into Q2 activities. This will require discipline and selflessness. It is worth it though because the rewards can be great. Spending more time effectively in Q2 many times will result in…

- Less crises because they have been prevented

- Happier family life because they have become an important part of your time and life.

- More productiveness and job success

- Better health and well-being

- Much less stress in all areas of your life.

So if you want a little short-term joy with little purpose in your life, Q3 and Q4 will help you achieve that. But if you truly want to discover purpose for your life along with long-term peace and joy, invest time into Q2. Perhaps you will need a true friend or trusted advisor to help you re-arrange your schedule and get on track for much better tomorrows.

POINTS TO PONDER

- Do you currently use a time management system and how is it working?

- Which quadrant do you spend most of your time in?

- What kinds of things are you doing that are Quadrant 2 activities?

- What can you change to allow you to spend more time in Quadrant 2?

Roger is a native of northern Indiana. After being raised on a farm, he graduated from Purdue University in West Lafayette, IN with a BS in Agricultural Engineering, and received his MSBA from Indiana University in South Bend.

He retired from a 30-year career at Laidig, Inc., a global manufacturing and construction company, as Sr. Vice President of Sales and Marketing, and is currently embarking in a part time position as an adjunct professor with emphasis in leadership at Purdue School of Technology in South Bend, IN.

Roger is the author of *Finding Purpose and Joy It's a Journey*, and provides one-to-one mentoring to men going through career and life transitions. Learn more about Roger at: http://www.findingpurposeandjoy.com

Resources:

About Brain Wave States
Excerpt from Hypnosis for Success

While most people are not particularly interested in how or why hypnosis works. For individuals with inquisitive minds, the process of hypnosis is fascinating. The brain goes through a series of changes during the process of hypnosis. The different stages are often referred to as depths. The five brain wave states experienced during the process are: beta, alpha, theta, delta, and gamma.

Under normal circumstances, a hypnotic experience begins in a beta brain wave state. Beta is our normal waking state and is associated with feeling alert. As with all of the brain wave states, beta frequencies range from low to high. Frequencies at the upper end of the beta range indicate stress, anxiety, and panic. The lower end of beta will accompany feeling alert, clear, and focused. Beta frequencies range from 14 to 39.9 Hz.

During the first phase of hypnosis, physical and mental relaxation is induced through a series of suggestions and instruction by the hypnotherapist. At this stage, brain waves slow down, entering an alpha frequency. The alpha state creates a feeling of detached awareness. During this brain wave state, an individual's memory, ability to learn new information, and physical senses are enhanced. It is common to experience vivid imagery and heightened sensations. Alpha frequencies range from 8 to 13.9 Hz. Although many significant changes can take place in an alpha state, research documents major therapeutic changes are possible while in deeper brain wave states.

Brain waves continue to slow down through the use of deepening techniques. Most hypnotic subjects will experience theta and delta frequencies. The theta state is renowned for accelerated healing and transformational experiences. Theta frequencies range from 4 to 7.9 Hz. Under normal circumstances, theta is achieved only momentarily, as you drift off to sleep and upon awakening. In hypnosis, this state allows for some of the deepest programming.

Delta waves are the slowest frequencies. They are typically experienced during deep sleep and very deep meditation. Delta frequencies range from .1 to 3.9 Hz. The delta brain wave state also contributes to accelerated healing, including healing from trauma.

After sufficient deepening, the hypnotherapist will shift into the therapeutic portion of the session. During this phase, the hypnotherapist will use various types of suggestions, guided imagery and metaphors which stimulate different parts of the brain. It is common for the client's brain wave states to fluctuate between alpha, theta and delta with short bursts of gamma waves throughout the therapy portion of the session. Gamma brain waves are the fastest of the brain wave frequencies. They indicate states of optimum or peak performance. Gamma frequencies range from 40 to 100 Hz. Gamma frequency is associated with flashes of genius and sudden bursts of insight.

At the conclusion of the hypnosis session, the hypnotherapist will gently return the client to a beta brain wave state. Because beta is our normal waking state, it is not possible to get stuck in a hypnotic state. Upon returning to a beta state, the client is still in a heightened state of suggestibility for up to three minutes.

Note: A self-hypnotic state, as in visualization exercises or guided meditation, is similar to those states experienced when working with a qualified hypnotherapist. However, you are less likely to enter deeper states (slowest brain wave states). Those who have trained themselves to go into long deep meditative states can enter the delta and theta brain wave frequencies more easily and regularly.

About the Author:

 Alicia Cramer is a mindset expert and professional business coach. She has been interviewed by Forbes Magazine, Fox and ESPN Business Radio and many others for her work with entrepreneurs and business owners.

Her passion for empowering others was evident at a very young age as was her desire to be an entrepreneur. Her own struggles with depression and self-worth issues eventually led to extensive research and application of mental conditioning techniques in conjunction with understanding Universal Principles and strategies for success.

Alicia attended college for marketing at the age of 18, and started her first business – an eCommerce store, at 22. That took her deeper into the field of online marketing where she dabbled off and on for years. Her journey was full of twists and turns, but her desire for entrepreneurship and the birth of her son cultivated her motivation to take business more seriously.

In 2010 she opened a hypnotherapy practice, which transitioned into a business coaching practice, specializing in mindset. Now Alicia passionately works one-on-one with entrepreneurs and high achieving individuals to overcome blocks to success in business and life.

Visit Alicia's website at: **www.aliciacramer.com**

"Alicia is one of the best in the game. Period."

Camelia Apostol, Artist

"Working with you has opened up so many things for me and the Universe is delivering wonderful things in response. Thanks for helping me get out of my own way!"

Linda Bucher, Life Coach

"It's hard for me to describe how easy self-discovery and self-improvement becomes when gently guided by Alicia. When I'm working with her, I never feel judged or exposed. This has allowed me to be completely honest with myself, and thus opened the door to my inner power and potential. Thank you Alicia"

Anabel Granados, Founder Steel Doll

"Alicia hones in where no words have reached to free up those feelings that I just could not get a hold of! She blows barriers like a stick of dynamite strategically placed to crumble mountains of disempowering beliefs."

Marlene Sanchez, CEO WarmGoods

An esoteric, yet practical guide for entrepreneurs who are unsatisfied with their current business to:

- ✓ Finally get clear on what you really want out of your life so can take practical steps to achieve it.

- ✓ Shift out of old disempowering belief patterns and habits, and into an aligned way of thinking and action for increased life and business satisfaction.

- ✓ Learn a simple and profoundly effective way to use the power of visualization to your advantage.

- ✓ Become proficient at recalibrating yourself to feel more empowered and be more effective in your business.

- ✓ Assess which high impact marketing strategies will work best for you to create your ideal lifestyle business.

About the Author: Alicia Cramer is business coach and renowned mindset expert. She works with small business owners and entrepreneurs to overcome mental and emotional obstacles to increased success, wellbeing and happiness.

Contributing Authors Include: Michael Schmidlen & Roger Laidig

ALICA CRAMER COACHING

www.ingramcontent.com/pod-product-compliance
Lightning Source LLC
Chambersburg PA
CBHW070843180526
45168CB00002B/944